This book is dedicated t... Entzminger & Cousin/ Be...

...over me.

I love & miss you both

Sheba

To my husband, family and friends thank you for always continuing to support me no matter what the endeavor is. I appreciate you! Elizabeth Entzminger, Cynthia King and Yvonne Brunson I love you all unconditionally and for different reasons. My inspiration to strive for excellence and beyond is because of you.

Table of Contents:

Introduction -02

The key to living a successful and happy life - - - --- - - - - - - - - - - - - - -09

Stopping yourself from destroying yourself - - - - - - - - - - - - - - - - - -26

Valuing yourself - 34

Recognizing your life triggers- 58

Setting goals and not taking failure personal - - - - - - - - - - - - - - - -68

Dealing with stress and stressful situations - - - - - - - - - - - - - - - - -76

Investing in activities that are meaningful and purposeful - - - - - -82

Learning to grow and being ok with getting support and help - - -88

Conclusion -94

Introduction

What really matters in life?

"The key to wisdom is knowing all the right questions." – John Simone

I simply love this quote. I believe that it really captures the entire wisdom of how to live a happy, joyful, successful and fulfilling life. Most of us go through life not really aware of their true potential. And that is the worst thing that could happen to any of us, because, we are all so unique, so strong and gentle at the same time, capable of almost anything we can set our minds to. It really bugs me that some people fail to see this; they fail to realize how strong they are, how powerful their minds are and how much they can accomplish in their lives! This book is dedicated to those people: the ones who feel like life has failed them, the ones who believe that they cannot change, and the ones who are unaware of their true potential. If you are one of them, please keep reading this book, and by the end of it, I promise you, you will have a completely different perception of whom you are and what you can accomplish in your life! You see, the truth in life is this:

We are what we perceive.

We are what we question and answer.

We are what we say.

We are what we feel.

We are what we do.

We are what we decide to be.

Moreover, our life changes together with our perception of the world, it changes with the things we say to ourselves, it changes with our feelings, it changes with our decisions and with the actions we take.

Let me ask you this: Have you ever noticed that small, bright, fiery spark in the eyes of wise people? If you haven't, please notice it the next time. And when you do that, please look even deeper into their eyes. Then, just for a second, you will see the invisible force that had driven them through the remarkable, hard, impossible situations in their lives. The same force that shaped their hearts, sharped their minds, and marked their souls. The one that made them walk when everyone screamed that they should stop, fly when they had no wings, speak when they had no words and go further, and lastly push harder when they had no strength. Doing it even with a smile. That force and power runs through everybody's veins. It defers from person to person, but its essence is the same. This force is the one that drives us to the boundary between good and bad, madness and wisdom, success and failure. If we chose to go ahead and follow it, it promises us hard work, long sleepless nights, adversity, love and wisdom. And if we are crazy enough and let that power to drive us through our lives, paint a smile on our faces and put kindness and love into our hearts, then and only then, we could say that we lived fully and truly. This power feeds from our love, drinks from our kindness and acceptance of others, it survives from our wish to move forward and create a better life, no matter how hard the world slaps us. Even though this force is really difficult to be explained, that is still not impossible. This force lies in each one of us. It is the life inside of us. Our way to stay in touch with the universe. In different cultures, it has different names: one call it soul, others faith, others call it intuition, some people call it ambition or desire to succeed, and I simply choose to call it our driving force.

Although this force lies within us, not all of us chose to follow it. Not all of us chose to let ourselves live a fulfilling life. In addition, for the situation to be worse, many of us even forget about ourselves. We put our desires, our hopes, and our dreams on the shelf and ignore them. We think about them every day but we ignore them. We always find some excuse and reasons why we cannot do it now, but that is the truth. By forgetting about ourselves, we make our self unhappy on purpose. At first reading, you may say, "this is ridiculous, why would anyone stop himself from being happy?" Well, the answer is simple: because of fear. Fear of failure, fear of not being good enough, fear of rejection, and fear of your own capabilities.

This is actually the reason why I decided to write this book. I wanted to let people know that everyone is capable of becoming successful; everyone is capable of living a fulfilling life. All they need to do is be a little braver and learn how to believe in themselves. Also making sure we are being mindful of our mental health.

I will start with revealing the secret of living a happy and fulfilling life, and what differs successful people from the one less successful. In here, we will talk about the healthy habits that these people have, how they differ from the others and what helps them live a fulfilled life. Then we will continue with the true purpose of this book: explaining to you how to improve yourself and with that, your life: we will begin with helping you to recognize your biggest problem, what is the thing that is holding you down? Why you keep making the same mistakes? We will also talk about how you can overcome your fears and stop yourself from destroying yourself. We will continue with the importance of valuing yourself and becoming a happy human being.

Once you know, once you get the impression of what you can achieve and why it is so important to start working on yourself today barriers can be broken. We will continue with explaining to you how to find your goal, recognize your life triggers and start working on yourself step by step. I will analyze thoroughly how to set goals and work on them, how to deal with the inevitable stress that is part of our every day life, how to stay positive after facing really stressful situations and finally how to invest in things you love and let your heart and soul grow. Lastly, we will talk about how to become ok with getting support and help. Knowing how to work on your relationships and create a better environment. A better life not only for yourself but also for the ones you love and are closest to you.

Always remember that you do not find a happy life – but you make it. And no matter how many storms get in your way, if you move forward with a happy spirit you will find that things always work out for those who work on themselves and give their heart and their soul into achieving their goals. So stop putting yourself on the backseat of your life. You're not helping anyone by doing that. Be the driving force, let yourself grow, and then, and only then will you see your true potential – that you can change your life and the lives of the ones that you love.

The key to living a happy and successful life

Every day you see people who are simply cheerful and full with life. You meet them in church, you meet them at your work place, when you go shopping, playing sports etc., and probably, at least once, you have said to yourself: "damn I wish I had his energy and enthusiasm, look how happy he / she is, his / her life must be perfect."

Well, let me stop you immediately and tell you something: their life is not perfect. No one's life is perfect – it is a fact. No matter how powerful you are, no matter "how high you are in the 'food' chain", what your rank is, or how much you get paid, no matter if you live in a big mansion and have a perfect family, you still can be unhappy and emotionally distant. Money and power does not buy you happiness. Family and big houses does not buy you tranquility. Happiness comes from within you. If you don't see that, you can never be happy. Being happy is not about having the perfect car, or the latest clothing, or biggest bank account. No! Being happy is actually realizing your value. It is about making peace with your inner self and realizing your value. Being happy is about not settling for anything less. It is about befriending your demons, your flaws and realizing that you are simply a human being. And what does this mean?

By befriending your demons, your flaws means realizing that you aren't perfect. None of us are. Even the greatest people, the stars that we look up to, our idols have flaws. Even they have something that they aren't proud of, and even they have made some mistakes. However, that does not make them any less worthy that only makes them human, and every human makes mistakes. What differs the happy and depressed person from one another is their attitude towards their mistakes. How they take failure. How they perceive it. And even more importantly, how they perceive happiness and success.

"If you can do what you do best and be happy, you are further along in life than most people." – Leonardo DiCaprio.

"Defining myself, as opposed to being defined by others, is one of the most difficult challenges I face." – Carol Moseley-Braun

"A smile is happiness you'll find right under your nose." – Tom Wilson.

"In every crisis there is a message. Crises are nature's way of forcing change — breaking down old structures, shaking loose negative habits so that something new and better can take their place." — Susan L. Taylor

"I don't have perfect teeth. I am not stick thin. I want to be the person who feels great in her body and can say that she loves it and doesn't want to change anything." And "I truly, truly believe that beauty is something that comes from within." – Emma Watson.

I felt obligated to share these quotes from some of the most famous people in the entire world with you to show you that true happiness is not about having everything figured out, but rather being satisfied with what you have and making a perfect plan on how to improve yourself and get the things you desire. Like Depp says, the problem is our attitude towards the problem. How we perceive it. How we understand it. How we let it affect us. How we search for solution. If you accept that in fact you will make mistakes, you will not be so hard on yourself. Therefore, instead of focusing on the problem, you will focus on finding the perfect solution and dealing with the situation – and that is the right attitude towards any problem in life.

If you wait for the perfect opportunity to come you will wait forever. If you wait to get the best paying job, create the perfect family and buy the biggest house you may still never be happy. Because believe me, when you get that job and create that family and buy the house you could still feel unhappy and unsatisfied. You want to know why? Because you will want more. Because it will not be enough. It will never be enough! The material things will not make you happy. Having a family will also not make you entirely happy. Only you can make you happy. If you feel unhappy with yourself, with what you do, that will reflect on you. That will reflect on your beautiful family too. What I am trying to say is not that you shouldn't go for the job you like. I don't mean that family is not valuable. No. I am not saying that at all. I am saying that you should not expect these things to magically make you happy. The true beauty is true happiness really comes from within – from realizing your value, from setting goals and working hard on them.

As human beings we will always want more, need more, search for more, and that is ok, that is in our nature. Nevertheless, before we reach for the stars and spread our wings, we need to learn who we are, what our heart truly desires and decide whether we will greet life with a smile or with anger. This knowledge is the thing that separates happy from unhappy people.

The secret to happy and successful life is the realization that happiness is not a thing to be discovered and acquired. It is not something that you can find externally or buy with money simply because it is not a possession to be acquired, but rather it is a state of mind. Happy people do not have everything that they want; they do not even have the best of everything. What they have is the right attitude towards the thing they do have and they make the best of whatever they have. They accept their mistakes, they accept their flaws, they never give up and they let themselves be satisfied. They are happy with the cards that life has dealt them and the way they have used them.

Happy successful people realize that they and solely they are responsible for their destiny. That they are responsible for their happiness. They are responsible for their success. They realize that each person is a unique human being with a different set of skills, dreams and mindset. Moreover, they are ok with that. They do not try to compare themselves with the rest and that's not how they "measure" their value. They do not feel the need to belittle someone to feel happy. In contrary, they realize that they are unique human beings and as so, they will always be great at something and bad at something too. More importantly, they realize that it is ok to be bad at something. If the artist constantly criticizes himself about not being able to draw well, he will never have time to focus on the thing that really matters in his life the thing that he is good at: art. Successful people realize that one of the key elements to happiness is finding out your purpose and living it out. Focusing on what really, truly matters the most to you. Sticking to your gut, your intuition, your calling, your soul. Being true to yourself.

Successful, happy people do not waste time on overthinking. They do not try to think of what can go wrong. They concentrate on positive thoughts. Even with identical life circumstances, unhappy people spend time thinking about unpleasant events in their lives, while happy people tend to seek and rely upon information that brightens their personal outlook. Unhappy people always view the problem as a problem. Happy people always look at the problem as another challenge – something that will help them grow, help them improve. They do not see the problem as a step back, but as a stepping stone to a better future. As another puzzle to which they need to find a solution. Most important of all, you can't be happy if you don't value yourself. Only people who know exactly how much they are worth, who work hard on becoming better versions of themselves, who believe that they deserve the best and respect themselves and accept themselves for who they truly are can achieve true happiness.

Happy people who value themselves, they follow instinctively these rules:

1. *They realize that they are the ones who bring the sunshine or the rain in their lives.*

As we discussed, the first step in becoming happy is realizing that you hold the key to your happiness and no one else. It is realizing that you control your happiness, your emotions, your decisions and your actions.

2. *Happy people who value themselves realize that they need to live in the moment*

Life is too complicated, too variable to worry about what will happen after a week or too. In a blink of an eye everything can change, so worrying about what future holds is unnecessary. Instead of focusing on what will happen next, what can go wrong, or simply what is next on their to do list, happy people focus on the task or conversation at hand. This way, they become more productive, more charismatic and likable.

3. Happy people who value themselves manage their energy

Our time is precious as well as our energy. So instead of engaging in pointless activities and wasting their time on useless thoughts that only exhaust our brain, happy people focus their energy on the things that make them happy, things that help them improve and become better versions of themselves. They learn how to remain calm and centered on the task.

4. People who value themselves focus on the positive side

Each morning when you wake up you decide what type of day this will be for you. Happy people realize that they have the power to be happy or unhappy. They realize that it is their decision whether they will start the day with being angry at their spouse about something that happened the night before and yelling at him first thing, or whether they will be glad that they have this lovely person in their lives, hug him, and continue working on communication and growing their union.

5. *People who value themselves do not lie to themselves*

Happy people realize that a little daydreaming can't hurt anyone, as long as it stays 'little'. This means that they accept having dreams, desires but they do not lose their minds over it. They do not wait for a miracle to happen and do not lie to themselves when the situation is bad. When they have a problem, they recognize it and not ignore it. They try to analyze it so that they can find the solution for it.

6. *Happy people who value themselves do not leave today's work for tomorrow*

Delaying your work problems will not help you solve it, rather it can make the problem even bigger. And happy people know it. There is a famous saying: Do not leave today's work for tomorrow. Delaying your work only creates anxiety; it floats over your head like a dark cloud making you angrier, more agitated, nervous about it, and in constant worrying of when it will be over.

7. People who value themselves realize that failure is not the end of the world

Many of us when faced some difficulties experience anxiety, and if they fail, they take it personal and believe that just because they have failed once; it will continue to happen forever. Well that is not true, and happy people know it. Again, we go back to their perspective and the way they see things: they do not see the failure as the end of the world, but rather as an opportunity to learn from their mistakes, improve and find better solutions, another way to success. Happy people see failure for what it really is: another stepping-stone that helps you on your way to success.

8. People who are truly happy and value themselves realize that if they are unhappy they can't make other people happy

We talked about how if you are unhappy your family and friends, wife, kids cannot help or force you to be happy. Only you can make yourself happy and the other people can only increase your happiness. Happy people know this and they are living by this rule. They care for others, but in doing so they do not neglect their own happiness. They let themselves grow and help other people grow too. They share their happiness. Share with the world the good experiences that life has blessed you with.

9. *They know that being good to themselves is crucial*

We spent our entire life with one person only. And this person is in our life from our birth to our death. No, it is not our mother, no, it is not our life partner, it is ourselves. Through good and bad, we only have ourselves. Happy people know this. They realize that people come and go from our lives. Some stay for few months, others for years some a bit longer, but eventually the only person on whom we can always count on is ourselves. Therefore, we need to be kind to ourselves just as we are with others. If you care not to hurt someone you love, you need to care not to hurt yourself too.

10. *They aren't afraid to show their feelings*

Are you feeling angry? Are you feeling lucky? Are you feeling joyful? Did something make you feel vulnerable? Happy people aren't afraid to show their feelings. They want the closest people around them to know what's on their minds and hearts. But here I don't mean you need to be a drama queen and exaggerate and end up talking solely about your feelings. I mean they know that others cannot read their minds, so they need to tell them if something is bothering them or makes them sad. Happy people know that expressing their feelings don't make them any less of a person, but rather it leaves space for others to see them for whom they truly are: a decent, kind human beings with feelings and emotions like everyone else.

11. *They show compassion to others*

Happy people know that showing compassion and understanding to how other people feel is not a sign of weakness but sign of mental strength, sign of good heart, kind soul and great spirit. To be able to recognize someone's feelings and help them feel better is one of the most important life lessons that each one of us should learn.

12. *They realize that belittling others won't make them grow*

One of our biggest problems that we as society face is bullying. Gossiping is not far behind too. Unfortunately, very often, the individuals who are being bullied when given the chance unconsciously become the bully themselves. This is the worst thing that can happen to any human being. Happy people know that saying something bad about someone, making them look bad in front of others won't make them a better person, but in contrary it will say more about themselves and their character instead of the people they are trying to belittle. Belittling others only makes one person little – the person that is saying the words. Aware of this, happy people tend to avoid and distance themselves from gossiping and belittling. They also try to avoid people who are prone to gossiping and belittling because they know that these individuals can't be trusted, and no one needs that type of person in their lives.

13. *They constantly step out their comfort zone and reach for new horizons.*

This is probably one of the main reasons for their happiness. You cannot be entirely happy in your comfy bubble. Know that happiness is just an illusion, a mask. We're meant to reach for the stars. We're created to dream and to make great things. Moreover, we can never do that wrapped up in our little falsely happy comfort zone. We need to grow, to learn new stuff, experience new things, and create new memories. Happy people know and strongly believe in this. They know how hard that first step out of your comfort zone is, because they have made it once previously in the past. In addition, they are thankful that they left their comfort zone, because around the corner of their comfort zone is the life they dream of and they can live it, solely if they dare to step out. There is an entirely different world waiting to be discovered, to be experienced right around the corner of your comfort zone.

Time to reflect

➢ Be honest to yourself. When you read all these characteristics that happy people possess, how many of them did you recognize yourself?

➢ How did this make you feel? Write down your feelings.

- Now that you have recognized yourself in solely a few of the characteristics of happy people it is time to make some changes. What changes will you be making?

Stopping yourself from destroying yourself

"He that is good for making excuses is seldom good for anything else." – Benjamin Franklin

Oh, how much truth lies in this sentence! If you are capable of making an excuse then you are definitely more than capable of helping yourself to become a better person!

In today's fast society when everyone is in a rush to do something, everyone is going somewhere, there is no time to waste, no time to spare, we all tend to lose the most important person in our lives – ourselves. Caught up the hurricane called life, desperate to make it on time with all the deadlines at work, pay the bills, finish the housework, help our children, further our education, have a social life and a decent six hours of sleep, we tend to forget how important we are to ourselves. This is the time when we start making excuses about why we cannot spare some time to do the things that our heart desires.

However, is this the real reason why we do not spare time to go after the things we dream of? Is really not having enough time the reason why we don't live the life we so desperately are in need of, I think that there is more to this. I think that time is simply a concept that we humans invented to make our orientation, our lives easier, but somewhere in the way, we lost the true reasons and started using it to make excuses. But what really lies behind our excuses? What is the thing that is destroying ourselves?

This thing, which has a name written with four simple letters, is actually the root of all the problems we as society are facing in global. This thing is fear. Fear has settled roots in many of our hearts and became our biggest enemy.

In this chapter, we will focus entirely on fear and how it is destroying us and what we need to do to stop it before it destroys us entirely. Let's begin with what fear really is.

Fear is the product of misunderstanding, lack of resources, information, experience and of course perspective. When one gets in the situation where he lacks all these things, he naturally begins to lack confidence. When the confidence is gone, so is the action necessary to achieve the goals that that individual has set for herself. This fear begins to grow and expand. Very soon, the person begins to make excuses about his life and circumstances all with desire to boost their self – esteem. Unfortunately, he is simply making the situation worse because the result is not what he have expected, in contrary the situation gets worse: the person gets trapped in an endless vicious circle - illusion of security. Instead of finding a permanent solution, the person keeps relaying on temporary excuses that not only are being useless but they also make the problem bigger.

With making excuses, the person ends up making the problem even bigger: he begins to lack responsibility and try to throw the fault to everyone but himself therefore stopping his personal growth. He ends up with limited beliefs about what he can and cannot do, starting to believe that he will never be good enough and that it will be better if he stops now and sticks to what is familiar to him. Locking himself into the vicious circle of false security the person starts creating his comfort zone that is limiting his view. He starts to have a pessimistic outlook on life and slowly begins to convince himself that everything is fine, although it clearly is not. The bad judgements followed by paranoia and of course regrets of huge proportions starts piling up on his door, and before he knows it, he ends up depressed.

So instead of preparing himself for a happy life filled with fulfilling activities and meaningful relationships the individual ends up isolated with pessimistic outlook on life, lack of responsibility, growth and deep self-doubt.

These are several types of excuses that we make and they all come from the several types of fear. As a person who wants to start valuing himself and stop putting himself on the back seat, and letting fear run his life, you need to learn the types of excuses that you make in your life and define what triggers them. Once you do so, then it will be easier for you to find the way to deal with your fear and focus on the things that really matter such as creating a better version of yourself, creating goals and achieving them.

There are many types of fears, but the ones that usually lurk in our shadows are:

Fear of change – the most common fear of all. People are always afraid of what they do not know and this is new to them. It is the thing that we are taught from the earliest age. But what we need to know is that change is a vital part of our lives and without change there is no growth.

Fear of failure – this is also very common and I myself have experienced it. This fear is reflected through the questions that every once in a while pop up in our heads and make a mess: "what if I fail? What if I'm not good enough? What if I make a fool of myself and don't finish the job?" This fear puts doubt in our abilities and it lowers our self – esteem. It forces us to look on ourselves through a broken mirror. But these words are delusion and the sooner we realize that, the sooner we will get rid of this fear and be able to live a happy normal life.

Fear of Embarrassment – No one wants to be embarrassed. Yet somehow, our society simply cannot put an end to the bullying, gossiping and making fun of each other. Usually embarrassment is not classified as fear, but rather fear comes as a result of an embarrassment. This fear in some cases is part of our lives from our childhood. When you get caught up doing something that is socially unacceptable or feel guilty about something and then someone publically reveals, "your secret" you get ashamed, made fun of, gossiped and in some cases even bullied. So afraid of this, you end up questioning everything you do and end up with fear of embarrassment.

Fear of making mistakes – this fear has destroyed so many lives and has deprived the world from so many talents. Fear that one will make a mistake, has made an individual not take initiation and do the things they want or dream of. We said it a few times by now and we will repeat it over and over until it becomes crystal clear: we are humans. We make mistakes; it is the way we deal with mistakes that really counts.

Fear of success – Yes, this is a fear, and although this may surprise you many people are afraid of success and what may come from it. I had a friend that because of fear of success turned down a promotion and has regretted it ever since. Afraid that he might not be good enough, that he may make a mistake and be held responsible afterwards, filled with self – doubt he refused the promotion. He said to me that all he was thinking was he would have more responsibility, have more duties and although that job was his dream he thought he wasn't good enough. It destroyed him. So many regrets followed, which in turn was unhealthy. So don't be afraid of success, run towards it!

These and the many other fears that exist and occasionally visit our minds, put tons of self – doubt in our hearts, confuse us and force us to make silly excuses that ruin our lives. If you want to grow and put yourself in first place, go for it. Not forgetting about yourself means taking a chance on you and investing in you.

Time to reflect

➢ Be fully honest to yourself. What are you settling for?

➢ What type of fears do you have?

➢ Analyze those fears. Are they real or they are irrational and exist only in your mind?

➢ Why do you have these fears?

Valuing yourself

This chapter is the heart of the book and we will explain to you everything in it – from what is valuing yourself, to the reasons why you should value yourself, to analyzing if you value yourself enough, the wrong ways to evaluate yourself and the right ways in which you can love, cherish and value yourself.

What is valuing yourself?

Valuing yourself means having respect, love and compassion for yourself. It means accepting yourself. It means working on yourself. One of the most important lessons in our lives is learning how to respect ourselves and understanding how to appreciate our worth.

Why you should value yourself?

With one sentence: because it defines who you are, who you are going to be and what type of life you will have. Your self-worth is a function of how you value yourself. Before others start appreciating your qualities, you first need to appreciate them yourself. Many people today are living an unsatisfied life filled with stress only because they do not see their true value and their true potential. In return they let others push them around and they accept jobs that they despise, even end up in relationships that make them unhappy solely because they do not respect themselves enough to realize that they deserve better. They need better and they most certainly can do better. But since they do not appreciate and value themselves enough they are unable to see that.

Valuing yourself is not an option it is a necessity.

People who value themselves know that their job, their relationships, their life goals need to make them feel happy and satisfied, not angry, anxious and unhappy. To value yourself means to value every second of your life and not letting time slip away from your hands.

People who value themselves are happy people. They know that they need to respect themselves enough to work a job that gives them some sort of fulfillment or do venture out and explore self-employment. Eight precious hours of our life every day we spend working. Eight precious hours that are never coming back. Multiply that by the days of the week, by the months in the year, by the years until you get pension. You will see that almost a quarter of your life will be spent on work. Don't let those hours go to waste by being unhappy. You would want to use them to make a mark on the world. To improve yourself. To become better. It goes with relationships too. People who value themselves respect themselves enough to walk away from anyone who no longer makes them happy. They believe, they know they can do better. Moreover, this is not some egotistic thing, no this is knowing that life is too short to be spent on meaningless work and meaningless relationships that bring nothing good.

Valuing yourself is important because it means taking your life in your own hands. Once you value yourself, you will never let other people dictate your life. Valuing yourself means not letting others tell you who you are, but you telling the world, better said, screaming at the world who you are. So many people have been bullied or have been in a relationship where they were used, their emotions were used and their dreams crushed. This affects us on a completely new level and it also affects the way we perceive ourselves. They may get the wrong idea about who they are simply because others said so and that is not good. Once you learn how to value yourself you will realize that people will always disappoint you, intentional or not, even the ones who love and care about you. And on some occasions you may even disappoint unintentionally the ones you love. You see, life is never going to be sunshine and roses, but just because you are going through challenges, does not mean that you have any more or less worth. You need to learn how to balance your life and never let yourself get lost. You need to learn how to forgive yourself and others without changing who you are and how you perceive yourself.

When you learn to discern between things you should place value in, and the things you should let go, your world will change. You will start to see the things around you differently. Once you start valuing yourself the world will begin to look different to you: you will no longer feel the need to explain yourself to anyone – you will feel confident in your own shoes and with every decision you make.

And more than enough times having confidence is crucial in getting the things you want. Your confidence is a key benefit you get from valuing yourself.

As I said, once you start valuing yourself you perceive everything differently. The glass that was half empty yesterday, today seems to you half full. You no longer see only the bad stuff around you, but you also see the good in the world too. You start to understand that it is ok to spare some time for yourself and once in a while put yourself even before your kids. You start to love the time you spare for yourself and start enjoying some new activities. With new activities, with new hobbies come new interests and of course new people. Once you feel confident in yourself, once you value yourself you will feel comfortable to approach everyone because you will no longer be afraid of what they will think about you or how they will perceive you. You will feel free to live your life and not be in constant fear and insecurity. Learning how to value yourself is not easy, it will be a long process in which you will have to invest your heart and your soul. You will need to be honest with yourself and embrace your flaws, deal with your mistakes and problems and learn how to face yourself and take responsibility. But once you start practicing it, you will never go back. You will realize that you deserve the best and you won't be able to be satisfied with anything less. And that will be the best gift you can give to yourself.

How **not** to value yourself?

When we talk about value of someone else, we usually start with their physical appearance, social status, money, material possessions, career and other outward appearances of success. But these aren't the things that define an individual. Usually the things that really define one person and are crucial in deciding whether we want him or her in our life is their inner, loftier values: love, integrity, kindness, emotional intelligence, forgiveness, compassion, inner balance, loyalty, truthfulness, and behavior. These things are actually the ones that matters, the ones that make one person better and the ones that define success and value. In order to value ourselves, we need to look inside us and search for these characteristics.

We will also never find self worth if we seek for it in someone else's approval. We will never find it if we evaluate ourselves by comparing our qualities with someone else's. Many of us, from a young age are taught that our self-esteem and our worth can be estimated by comparison and by competing. Most people, if they are asked and they answer truthfully, will admit that they believe they are above average and better than others on almost every trait. This is a delusion that masks the painful feelings of inadequacy. Moreover, although it masks the feelings of inadequacy it does not help us, it comes with high price of hurting us! When you evaluate your self-worth through comparing yourself with others, you start competing against others and this starts putting seeds of doubt deep within yourself. Furthermore, social comparison and competition always leads to disconnection with other people and change the way you see other people: you begin to look at them as obstacles that need to be overcome in order to keep your position and be the best. And this only brings trouble in our minds and hearts because the competition where only one person is the winner leads to the feeling of separation. We become distant from others and we avoid our primary goal as a human being – the desire to belong and be loved.

This comparison also leads to other demons – misery, self – criticism, fear and excuses. When faced with criticism, we become defensive and feel crushed. If the other person turns out to be slightly better than us in something, that immediately crushes the way we look at ourselves, because when valuing yourself through comparison you see yourself as the ultimate winner, the better person, and when that changes, your entire self- worth, your entire evaluation falls into water and you end up with a broken heart. You start over analyzing, the mistakes and failure start making you insecure, the anxiety becomes your prison and every time you face challenge in the future, you end up being stressed. This further reduces your chances of winning, and if you lose that challenge again then you end up on the way to low self – esteem. So your entire picture of who you are changes in just a second and you get the wrong impression about yourself just because you have lost one or two wars – things that happen to every single one of us and is completely natural.

With this type of self-valuing the result is one: we ultimately feel more separate from others and end up feeling hurt, worthless and full with self-pity. Instead of becoming better and reaching for the stars, we end up with hurt egos, broken self-esteem and no self-respect.

Many researches have confirmed that the competitive self – esteem is closely tied to larger social problems, such as loneliness, isolation and even prejudice. So, instead of helping you become a better person and realizing your true potential, this type of self – esteem only helps you get the wrong picture of who you are and sooner or later it ends, and you end up being hurt and dragged into anxiety.

How to value yourself

There is a reason why it is called self-worth and self-respect, because you need to do it YOURSELF. Self-worth can never come from someone else or from some material possession; it can only come from within you. The process of learning how to value yourself and stop taking your feelings for granted, the process of learning how to always remember yourself always begins with honesty.

You need to decide that you deserve your own time. You need to remind yourself of your own existence. Learning how to stop forgetting about yourself. You can be either your biggest cheerleader or your worst enemy. If you decide that you want to be the best version of yourself and value yourself you need to start learning how to do so now.

The first thing you need to know is what is self-respect, self-worth and self-esteem. We often use them in the same connotation but they do not have the same meaning. Self-respect, as the name says clearly, means having respect for your own self, for your character, desire, for your dreams. The self-esteem compared with the self-worth is more about confidence and healthy admiration for one's self. On the other hand, self – worth is the crucial part of mental and emotional health. It is more connected with knowing your value and it always come from within. The best thing about self-worth is the fact that you and only you have control. Meaning you are the one who puts value on yourself and you decide whether you will let and how much you will let the outside factors to influence your inner sense of value. By the outside factors here we mean other people's actions, opinions, judgements, reactions, their expectations and demands. Basically, everything that is coming from the outside, from society's unspoken standards to the rules written on paper, to the desires and expectations of our loved ones and the demands of our job. The reason why we first spoke about how not to evaluate yourself was precisely this. I wanted you to know how risky it can be for you to value yourself based on external sources.

1. Be honest

Once you know what self-value, self-worth and self-esteem are, and you know how important they are and how you should not evaluate yourself, you begin to focus on the right way to value yourself; the right self-valuation always starts with honesty. You can never have true self-evaluation if you aren't entirely honest with yourself. This is the first step and the most painful part because it means facing your inner demons. Being honest with yourself means standing up in front of the mirror and looking, really looking at yourself. Be honest about who you are. Be honest about what you desire. Be honest about what you have. Be honest about what you want to have. Be real with your desires, don't expect miracles to happen overnight, because when they don't happen you will end up disappointed. We will talk about how to be real more when we talk about setting goals and achieving them.

2. *Embrace your mistakes*

It means being honest about your mistakes. It means realizing that you aren't perfect – no one is. More importantly, it means accepting that you have made mistakes and that it is ok. It is ok to make mistakes. It is ok to accept the fact that you will probably make them again. But as long as you give your heart and your soul, and try to do the right thing it doesn't matter. You are who you are, with all your virtues and flaws. You have become who you are because of these virtues and flaws. By accepting your flaws, it does not mean that you should let them grow. By this, I mean accepting that you were responsible for those mistakes, facing the feelings of guilt and shame and accepting the fact that you cannot change the past, but you sure can change the future and how you will handle similar situations in the future. Analyze the situation truthfully, and ask yourself what was the reason that you reacted that way? What were you feeling, what made you so angry and why? Then, breathe and try to understand your reasoning, and more importantly was it rational or were you guided by your feelings and let your ego run the show. If you had a time machine and went back to the past, would you do the things again the same way or would you do something differently? Once you resolve this, accept the fact that it was what it was, learn your lesson from it and seal that case. Don't let yourself get lost in the past. Move on with a smile.

3. *Stop delaying*

My mom always used to say, "Today's work is not meant for tomorrow." She was right. If you delay your work, you only create bigger stress. It keeps floating above your head like a dark cloud and does not give you a chance to be happy. My friend has this simple yet amazing rule: "If the job takes less than 10 minutes, do it immediately." If you want to get something done, it will probably take 10 or 15 minutes top, do it now, do delay it.

4. *Stop making excuses*

The other mistake that we all are guilty of and that is fatal for our self-value is making excuses. In the first few pages, we went through the types of fears that stand behind making excuses. Now I feel like we need to spare some time for the types of excuses we make and how we need to handle them. They have a lot of influence over the way we perceive ourselves. Here are some of the excuses that we use often, what they really mean and how you can avoid making them:

Excuse number one we use is we do not have enough time! It is the most ridiculous excuse of all because time is just a concept invented by us humans to make our lives easier but it actually makes us more complicated. This excuse in translation means that you aren't focused enough; you lack passion, direction and discipline.

Furthermore, it means that you aren't managing your time effectively and that your priorities aren't where they need to be. This excuse can also mean that you simply do not value your time or just do not want to take the time to do what you feel you must in order to achieve your goal or in other words – you are lazy. And laziness is definitely not how you want to define and value yourself. The next excuse that we often make that hurts a lot of our self – esteem is "I don't know how, or I don't have an education, I'm not qualified enough." This excuse really hurts yourself because after a while you start seeing yourself as someone who is not good enough and you convince yourself in the lie you have told simply because you have lacked belief and confidence in your own abilities and you lacked creativity, inspiration and desire. This excuse is not only bad for your self-esteem but also for your reputation and for how other people perceive you. Because if you can convince yourself that you aren't good enough then you can convince others too. The next time you feel like making this excuse, remind yourself that you are a capable human being made from the same material as the others.

The only thing that you lack is practice and education and you can get them easily. Especially today, in the era of technology you can easily find some course and learn the things you have missed out on. Do not let yourself feel not good enough just because you don't have a certain level of. It is just a piece of paper and there are many multi-millionaires and billionaires who have nothing more than a high school education and some of them don't even have that. If you don't know something and how it needs to be done, ask someone who does there is no shame in that, someone taught them how to do it too, they weren't born with knowledge. If there is no one you can ask, go on the internet. There are so many courses, so many online schools that can help you achieve your goal. Believe in yourself, believe that you can achieve anything that you set your mind to. Stop making excuses and hurting your self-esteem.

The next excuse that people make that hurts their self-esteem really bad is: "I can't change." That is not true. In fact, it is the furthest from the truth! You can change; we all change all the time.

Maybe you don't see it, but you do change. Some change more, some less. It is in our human nature to grow, change and improve. What you consider unable to change is simply lack of motivation and reason to change. Moreover, this suggests that you lack emotional pain that would help you to accelerate change. If you do not believe you can change, the reason for this is that you simply have not associated enough pain to not changing. Once you begin to look at all the dire consequences that will result from not making a change, then you will soon realize that the motivation was always there. All you need to do is ask the right questions: What will happen, how will this affect my life, if I do not make this change? Will I regret it? How will it make me feel? On which fields in my life will this change have effect: will it affect my health, my career, and my relationships? Is my consistency and stubbornness really worth the price that I will pay if I do not change? Once you start thinking seriously about these questions, you will start finding motivation to make the change.

Excuses are bad in every possible aspect for us. They hurt our self – esteem and they hurt our image, so avoid making them as much as possible.

5. *Understand your true power of your attitude towards yourself*

This is probably one of the most valuable, crucial lessons in learning how to value yourself. You must understand that the way you perceive yourself, the way you represent yourself and talk to and about yourself eventually becomes the real you. So, if you constantly put yourself in second place, others will start to put you in second place too. If you start over criticizing yourself, belittling yourself and not recognizing your good qualities solely talking about your flaws, you will end up being perceived as someone not worth both by yourself and other people. On the other hand, if you start making everything about yourself, if you exaggerate your qualities, talents, and skills, if you try to make everyone worship you and everything you do, you will come across as egotistical and arrogant. Furthermore, almost always, behind the over-estimating your self-worth stands insecurity and fear of rejection. Therefore, both belittling and exaggerating of your qualities and skills is a bad thing. You need to have the right attitude toward yourself. You need to stay honest and truthful. You need to look at yourself and be able to see the real you.

6. Be gentle to yourself

Don't over criticize yourself and be careful with the way you talk to yourself. When you are surrounded with people or when you talk to your closest friends or family, you don't insult them or belittle them because you don't want them to feel bad and get angry at you. So why would you talk badly with yourself? Be gentle with words, you spent your entire life with yourself, don't make it a bad journey filled with negativity. Like I said, we eventually become what we tell people we are and what we work on, so work on yourself, tell yourself good things, dream, be gentle, be honest and let yourself grow.

7. Don't worry about being accepted by others

What others think of you is none of your business. We talked a lot about how bad it is to compare yourself to others and measure yourself in that way. Well, it is as fatal if you let other's opinion be your measurement of your self-worth. You must realize that every single person in this world is unique and that is what makes us so special. Every single person you meet is different and in on a unique path – he or she is also at a different place in his growth and development. Furthermore, only that person knows about the struggles in his life, just like only you know about the difficulties and the problems, as well as the joy in your life. So do not worry about not fitting in someone else's picture of perfection. You need to fit only in your own picture. Don't be afraid to be unique, celebrate your uniqueness. One of the most powerful steps towards truthful self-evaluation and learning how to love yourself is learning how to be true to yourself and not to be afraid to express your needs, desires and dreams just because others do not see it the way you do. If something is important to you, do not be afraid to ask for it, don't be afraid to tell others how you feel. You deserve to be happy with yourself, you deserve to love yourself for who you are and let others love you for who you are from the inside. "We are all wonderful, beautiful wrecks. That's what connects us–that we're all broken, all beautifully imperfect." – Emilio Estevez

8. *Spare time for the activities you love*

Just like we are all unique human beings with unique characteristics and life stories, we also have unique desires. We like to think that we are all alive for a reason. Also, having a life purpose is what makes our soul tremble, our heart sing and our pulse rise. Purpose and meaning is the foundation for self-worth as it gives us a reason for living. It is the thing that drives us, the fuel that keeps motivating us, inspiring us to keep going, pushing our boundaries and becoming better. It keeps the enthusiasm and hope alive in our hearts. So always spare some time to pursue your dream and do the activities you like.

9. *Live in the moment, do the best with what you have and move on*

I really admire my mom. Once I got older, I realized how I should live my life. My mom doesn't rush. She is satisfied with what she has, and every single day she likes to strive to do better and work on improving herself. I know this at first seems out of topic but trust me it is not. Often in the entire chaos around us, tangled between work, home, kids, family, and partners we forget not only about ourselves but also about the little things in life that make life great. We take our youth for granted. We take our home for granted. Moreover, we forget that this moment will never repeat itself. You will never be as young as you are now; you will never feel the same. So each day spare at least a few seconds to admire nature. To work on your health. To enjoy your morning coffee. To tell your partner, your kids, your parents, your friends how much they mean to you. Do not waste your precious time thinking about the past, the regrets you have or the plans for the future. This moment, right now, is the most important time of your life. Every single day use the resources you have, give your best at your job and once the work is done, you are out of your work place, stop thinking about it.

You have done the best you can and that is enough. You will value yourself more if you value your time, your memories and your surroundings.

10. Be grateful for what you have

To value yourself also means to value the things you have. To value your time. If you value yourself you also value the people that are in your life because they help you become a better person and are there for you no matter what.

11. Trust your own feelings

At the beginning, we talked about that feeling that is inside of us, that driving force that makes us who we are. Well, self-worth requires you to learn to listen and rely upon your feelings, as we say, to go with your intuition, or go with your gut. The great thing about trusting your intuition is that it helps you to stop forgetting yourself. When the demands are placed upon you and you don't feel great and you want to respond with what works better for you or both of you instead of simply trying to satisfy everyone else's needs, you start realizing your worth and that you matter. Your opinion matters. And your feelings help you to realize that.

Time to reflect

- ➢ Be honest with yourself. Do you value yourself enough?

- ➢ Is there anything that makes you feel uncomfortable in your skin? What is that and can you change it?

- ➢ Do you make excuses and why? Why do you have those excuses?

Recognizing your life triggers

What are life triggers? I believe there are two types of life triggers: one that motivates us and give us strength, and the other is emotional triggers that weakens us and bring storms into our lives. In this chapter we will try to analyze the emotions that each one of us face on a daily basis, try to classify them, find out what triggers them and how we can control them and use them to grow and become a better person.

There are two types of motivation: external and internal. Promise of some kind of reward, or promotion, can motivate one person. These types of motivations are external because they come from an outside source. External motivation although to some may seem like not real motivation is still a motivation and can still inspire people to create a goal and work hard on achieving it. For example, if you are working in a company and the owner, or the manager says that the new project that you and the others will work on is vital for the company and the person who finds the perfect solution and presents it will get promotion, this for sure will inspire you to work harder to get a promotion. This type of motivation comes from an outside source – or in the case of our example from the manager/boss. Sometimes, we don't need other people to inspire us, although the price that motivates us may still be the same. We have established the sources of motivation, more precisely who can motivate us, but we have not said the reasons, what really motivates people on a deeper level. Well, many psychologists claim that what really motivates people and has proven to be the most powerful motivators are achievements and the recognition of that achievement. These two always go hand in hand because without achievement, the recognition is simply empty, and without recognition, the achievement is rarely rewarding.

We said that there is external motivation and we explained how others could motivate us, but now the question is how can motivate ourselves. Let's be real, in today's world we can easily get distracted and feel unappreciated. Moreover, sometimes, we simply cannot wait on others to inspire us, in fact, we should not wait on others to inspire us, we should do it ourselves. Nevertheless, how can we inspire ourselves to do something? How can we motivate ourselves?

The first step in motivating yourself is to write the reasons on paper. Write down why you want something. Writing down will help you by making it easier to track your progress and stay motivated. When you have written the reasons and manage your progress you will be aiming towards more real, more 'visible' goals and this will help you stay motivated longer than simply aiming for an abstract goal. One crucial thing that will hold motivation in its hands is reality. This means you need to stay real. Your goals need to be achievable, and I would definitely recommend you to start small and stay real to yourself, your character and your desires. This means that if you hate something, even if you write it down and stay small, you won't be motivated by it simply because you hate it and this will only create additional stress. Also practice rewarding. Kids aren't the only ones who love rewards, and rewards can turn out to be a great motivator. For example if you are on some strict diet, after a while when you achieve your goal and lose part of the weight, as a reward give yourself a treat. This will motivate you to stay on task but yet reward yourself for doing good.

The next step in staying motivated is stopping fear before it stops you. We talked about fear and excuses already and you know the damage they can do to your self-esteem. These two can also inflict unspeakable damage to your motivation too. So do not let fear stop you, control your fears by always staying real, rational and true to yourself.

Do not be afraid to search for motivation in some other places. I know that many people will think it is corny, but creating a playlist with songs that are positive, give you good vibes and make you feel happy, comfortable and joyful and at the same time they inspire you and also help you to stay motivated. It goes with finding some inspirational quotes or reading some motivational books, or some inspirational positive e-books that will help you stay positive and motivated. You can also start a motivational journal, and as we said write down your progress, or you can use a calendar and mark it every single day, there is nothing more satisfying than hitting a check sign at the end of the day in your achievement calendar. You can even schedule weekly check-ins and see how your progress is going, analyze what is going good, what not so good and how you can improve.

The last way in which you can get motivated is to involve your friends or partner in your motivation. This could be a great idea especially if the goal you are trying to reach is something that you two have in common. Then you can work on it together and help each other stay in check, resist the temptations and continue being motivated.

The other types of life triggers that we mention are the emotional triggers and these are usually the storms in our lives. The emotional triggers are the things that set off a memory tape or a flashback transporting us back to the event of our original trauma. You cannot value yourself if you do not really know yourself. And in order to get to know yourself you need to know what makes you smile, what makes you cry and what makes you happy. You need to understand your emotions, you need to find what triggers you. Now the process of discovering what really triggers you can be really challenging, but once you realize what triggers you, you will be able to understand your emotions and yourself better and it will help you heal faster. Furthermore, once you learn what triggers you, you will be able to also learn how to deal with your emotions and cope better in the future.

The triggers have huge roles in our behavior and how we perceive ourselves. Before we start explaining how you can recognize your life triggers, let's first explain why we all have them. Triggers are actually our way of coping with the past. In simple words, the reasons why we have triggers is because we were all once children who while growing up have experienced some negative emotions, more precisely pain or suffering and because we were kids, we couldn't acknowledge those feelings and / or deal with them properly. As a result that pain found it is place in our brain, in some memories, and when we grow up and become adults, and experience something similar to the event from when we were children, it triggers our emotions. And what do we do then? Well, since humans are creatures of habit, we typically turn to a habitual or an addictive way of trying to manage painful feelings.

Example if you were neglected in your childhood, you had busy parents or didn't spend enough time with them because of some reason, they were unavailable to you, when you grow up, you may start to overreact when someone isn't available to you. Another example when you call your friend and she does not answer because she was busy or when your boyfriend does not return your call. You may do this, and consider it other people's fault, without realizing that your real problem lies with your emotional trigger – in this case, "unavailability." Since you were neglected as child, you try to avoid the old pain by blaming your friends or boyfriend. However, once you discover your trigger, find what 'match' triggers a fire in your heart, you can easily learn how to control it and not let it affect you so much where it dictates your behavior.

But how can you discover what really triggers you? What makes you feel vulnerable? Let's complete a few simple exercises from which you can learn what triggers your emotions;

1. Close your eyes. Imagine that you are arguing with someone you love, for example a friend, a family member or a boyfriend. Why do you guys argue? What did they do to make to feel you so angry? What is the problem, what thing made you lose control? If you can find it, you know what your trigger is.

2. Look at the list of the most common emotional triggers that I have presented to you bellow. Do you react immediately if it is one of these things you aren't getting and it is very important to you?

Acceptance	Be needed	Comfort	Predictability
Attention	Be in control	Freedom	Safety
Autonomy	Be right	Fun	Variety
Balance	Be understood	New challenges	Love
Be liked	Be treated fairly	Order	Included
Be valued	Consistency	Peacefulness	Respect

Now, be entirely honest. Which of these emotions, or more precisely the lack of which of these triggers your emotions? Choose at least three items from the list that most often set off your emotions. You need to understand that needs aren't bad, the reason why you have these needs lies in the fact that at some point in your life that particular need served you. It made you feel better. What is bad is you being attached to these needs more and more. When this happens, your brain starts searching and is on the lookout for circumstances, which may have treated your ability to have these needs met. This process is the process of creation of emotional triggers.

When you discover your emotional triggers, you must stop and think very carefully and analyze the entire situation. Stop for a second, don't jump to conclusions and don't let the anger get the best of you. Relax, breathe, release the tension in your body and clear your mind of all thoughts. Then focus on your feelings, how you feel, how you want to feel or who you want to be in that precise moment. In addition, you must be completely honest with yourself; ask yourself whether the person actively is denying your need or you are simply overreacting? If you are overreacting, stop what you are doing and apologize. If you aren't, then think whether you can ask for what you need or if you cannot do that, then ask does it really matter or can I let it go? If it does mater than speak openly about it with the person.

Time to reflect

- ➢ What are your triggers?

- ➢ What do you do to manage the painful feelings that are triggered?

- ➢ Do you face your triggers or try to avoid the pain and stick to bad habits?

Setting goals and not taking failure personal

In the dictionary, you will find the following definition of goals: "Goals are the result or achievement toward which effort is directed; aim; end;" And although this definition is true, and you can use it to explain to someone what goal means, when we say what are goals we mean what effect does goals have on us? Why are they important?

The goals are our hopes, our dreams for the future. They are our fuel. Our hope. Every person who has achieved something in their lives has set a goal first and worked on it. Setting goals gives you long-term vision and short-term motivation. It focuses your acquisition of knowledge, and helps you to organize your time and your resources so that you can make the very most of your life. We have three areas of goals: based on time, focus and topic. Based on time is where we have goals that are planned to be achieved in a short period of time and goals that take longer period of time to be achieved: short-term and long-term goals. For example, a short-term goal may be learning or passing an exam, while the long-term goal may be finishing college. The next category is focus. These goals are the goals that drive majority of our decisions. It effects many of your personal and professional decisions – meaning you have to adjust and adapt your personal and professional decisions in the way that helps you achieve the focus goal. Finally, based on the topic, we can have personal, professional, career and financial goals. Most of our goals aren't mutually exclusive but they are rather related. For example if your goal is to completely change the way you look (your focus goal which at the same time is a long-term goal) then you also set several short-term goals that will help you achieve that goal. For example, your short-term goals in this case may be to save money so you can afford a trainer, to go to a fitness gym to lose weight, or to plan a diet and lose weight;

From a young age we're all taught that we need to have some goals in life: to build a career, get married, buy a house, get into good college and so on. Setting goals is a crucial, vital part of our lives because it helps us to give purpose to our lives. Goals give meaning to our lives. They motivate us to wake up in the morning and go to work. Not having goals is like getting on a train which has no final destination. The purpose of the goal is to achieve something that will help you become better, become more successful, more powerful, or simply more happier, more satisfied with your life. Not having a goal means not having a light in the dark, so you keep walking and walking not aware of where you are, what to do next. Without goals we feel not good enough, because we see all the people around us working on something, trying to achieve something and we are here doing nothing and it makes us question ourselves and our self-esteem. Every single person has unique desires, unique dreams and therefore, unique goals.

How to set a goal? The first step in setting a goal is deciding what you want to do or work towards. It can be a personal goal, such as improving your blood pressure, budgeting, or a career goal such as taking course or goal related with work – it doesn't really matter what it is as long as it is something that you really want to do and you know it will help you and make your future better. Start with something smaller and let yourself rise. The next step is to make a plan and write it down. Write down your reasons, write down why you need to succeed, what this goal will change for you, and how it will affect you. However, be careful. Your goal needs to be real, you cannot reach for something that is unreal because that way you will end up being hurt and disappointed. So be honest with yourself and set real goals. In addition, the timetable, the time you give yourself to achieve your goals needs to be real. Otherwise, you can lose motivation and with that lose pace of your goal. Make the plan detailed, don't just write two sentences but explain how it makes you feel now, how it will make you feel later. What changes will it bring to your life? And go in details when describing your goal. Focus on the terms, on the rules to which you will stick to while working on your goals.

On your way to achieving your goal you may have trouble, you may face some obstacles. In these situations, it is important to stay motivated. Go to your journal read once again the reasons why you decided to set that goal in the first place. Talk with someone who is there for you who will try to understand you and give you real, useful advice. Find some advices online or again, search for additional motivation online, in some books, or songs. If you feel like you are going to make a mistake and walk away from your path that leads to your goal, take a step back and relax. Do not jump to conclusions while you are under the influence of your feelings because you will regret it later. I personally, always practice sleeping before making some big decision. Once you sleep and wake up your brain is back to normal, you are refreshed, relaxed and you can think about the problem you are facing with a clear head and make a rational decision that you will not regret later. Even if you lose one battle, you need to remember that losing a battle does not mean losing the war. You cannot always win, sometimes you may lose some wars. You see the main thing that differs the winners from the losers is the way they deal with failure. The way they accept defeat. Strong people who believe in themselves know that failure should not be taken personal. They know that failure is just another step that leads to success. If you fail 100 times, you need to stand up 101 times. If you want to succeed, like I said you need to change your perception. You need to change your self-esteem, as we talked, and you need to change the way you perceive failure.

Remember, failure is nothing personal; it is just a natural, inevitable part of life and success. From a child's point of view, if a child starts to doubt himself and stops trying, he will never learn the basics of life: how to walk, how to talk. Instead, it takes it slowly and eventually reaches its goal. Now, you should feel the same about failure: it is nothing personal, just another step that will help you reach your goal. If you look at failure better, you will realize that failure is not even that bad, and that it can help you succeed. Here is how failure can help you: failure will help you redefine your goals. It will show you what you are doing wrong, how you should proceed and what is your mistake. Failure helps you to stay realistic. It will keep you grounded. If you learn from failure, you will be able to redefine your methods and come one-step closer to succeed. Moreover, failure can also turn out to be one hell of a motivator, it can help you stay focused and motivated on finding a solution. It will be a reminder of the things you did wrong and if you learn from it, it will prevent you from doing them again in the future. Stop seeing failure as your enemy and start seeing it as your teacher. As something that exists to show you the right way, something that will help you grow, learn from your mistakes, improve your methods, become a better person and achieve your goals.

Remember, you are the one holding your life cards, you decide every single morning whether you will be brave enough and reach for the stars or if you will stay in your comfort zone. And before you make the decision know that the decision you make today defines your tomorrow.

Time to reflect

- What is your goal in your life?

- Have you had any goals in your past, and did you achieve them or you didn't? Why do you think your previous goals were successful / failed?

- Define at least 3 goals that you would like to achieve this year.

- How do you perceive failure?

- In what ways have you dealt with failure previously in your life?

- What can you change to achieve your goals this year?

Dealing with stress and stressful situations

At first hearing, stress and self- value seem to be not quiet related, nevertheless, they are much more related than we could ever imagine. In fact, if you look closely they are tightly connected with each other. How one deals with stress has a lot to do with their self-value and perhaps in order to start dealing with stress more efficiently, we should first work on how we perceive ourselves.

Now a days we aren't only living in the era of technology, but we are also living in the era of stress and anxiety which is exactly why it is important to improve our self-esteem and be able to deal with stress more easily.

To be honest, when I was younger I was not very confident in my own skin, I always thought that I wasn't good enough and that other people around me were much better than I was. In fact, that was one of the main things that was making me stressful. I used to walk around thinking that everyone was judging me and my flaws and although deep inside I knew that that wasn't true, I couldn't avoid it or with other words- I couldn't help myself.

Every time I was experiencing anxiety or stress, I wasn't telling myself something nice in order to calm down, but instead I was constantly thinking about all my flaws, constantly examining what is wrong with me and why certain things were happening exactly to me. I thought that probably I am the only person in the world that was going through the things I was going through and that I was the only person in the world that was feeling what I was feeling. That perception that I had about myself and my life was just increasing my anxiety more and more.

Nevertheless, as I grew older things significantly changed. I started reading more articles about how someone could improve their self-esteem and how to deal with stress and I realized that every single issue in this world has a solution, yet that solution is not something that will come by itself, but it has to come only from myself.

I realized that the key I was looking for so long was in myself and that my own thoughts and my perception about my personality and my life were the things that could decrease my stress and improve my life.

I came to the realization that every single person in this world is going through or has gone through the same or similar things that I was going through back then. Realizing that, that was not only normal, but it was even helpful in order to make people grow and mature, to make them stronger and smarter. And I did grow stronger and wiser because I realized that only I am the one who is in charge of my own life and my own struggles.

Despite that, stress did not completely go away, but knowing how to cope with it- makes, stress way less powerful than it was before.

Now every time I am going through stressful situations I remember how grateful I am for everything I have in life. I try to remember that now I am way stronger than I was before thanks to all the difficult situations that life was putting me through and although stress doesn't really go away, it doesn't have so much power over me anymore.

Maintaining a positive outlook is perhaps the crucial thing that one should do in order to deal with stress successfully. Instead of being attacked of negative thoughts when going through stressful situation, now I am protecting myself with positive affirmations about life. Reminding myself that no matter what happens in life, I could always get up and carry on is perhaps my major strength. Life always gives other chances if we want to take them. Knowing that is so important to keep me moving even when I don't feel like it.

Another important thing that I always do when I go through stressful situations is focusing on the progress that I have made. No failure could erase all my progress that I have made before and knowing that I have made that progress once only reminds me that no matter what happens I can make that progress again and come out from the issues as a way stronger and more mature person. Failure or stress is actually another type of life lesson that although it is not that nice, we all have to learn and truth to be told, there is always a lot to be learned from failure.

It teaches us how to be more confident in our own skin and how to fight as a soldier every time we fall down. It teaches us that what we give power to, has power over us or, at least, that' what it has taught me.

All in all, how is one is dealing with stress and how one perceives themselves are two things that are tightly connected to each other because everything comes from our mind.

Stress is not that powerful if one knows how to cope with it and coping with stress would be impossible if one doesn't know their self-value and doesn't feel confident in their own skin.

On the other hand, if a person knows their value and strength, that person is like an army that could never be conquered. Affirmations and reminders of all our progress are two things that could slightly improve a human's self- esteem and give them strength every time they think they are losing it. Another reminder that could significantly boost one's self-value and self-esteem is that every thing in this life happens for a reason. If that reason is not good enough to make us happy then it is definitely good enough to make us stronger and more mature than we were before. Maybe stress, after all, is not always a negative thing, maybe it is just a tool to give us strength and make us grow in an emotional way.

Lastly, when dealing with stress one should never forget that life always gives second chances. Whenever, one is going through a stressful situation, thinking that there is no solution for their issue, they should only think that no matter how many times they fall, they could always get up and give it another try. With the right affirmations, the right thoughts or the right mindset, stress is just a word that does not have much meaning. Trusting in our own abilities, our own will and our own strength is our major weapon against stress.

Stress gets scared every time it meets a person who keeps the positive outlook and never stops trying to make it through it is way as a stronger and wiser person. I have experienced that in my own skin and I know that each one of us has that potential, each one of us has the potential and the strength to conquer stress only by knowing how valuable and how strong we are.

Time to reflect

- What are the situations that stress you the most?

- How do you deal with stress?

- Is your way of dealing with stress a useful one and what can you do to improve it?

Investing in activities that are meaningful and purposeful

"The greatest gift you can give someone is your time. Because when you give your time, you are giving a portion of your life that you will never get back." This is one of my favorite quotes of all time, and although I do not know who said it, I believe in every single word of it. Our time on this planet is limited. That is why we need to spend every second of our life doing things that fulfill us, that make us happy, that brings joy to our lives, draw a smile on our faces and help us become better, stay healthier and be one-step closer to achieving our goals.

There will always be something new that you can learn that will help you improve your life. Your adulthood is the perfect time to do so because without the pressure of parents or school you will still be able to discipline and motivate yourself to learn the essentials. These meaningful and purposeful activities will help you rise to your horizons. In addition, getting in activities that are meaningful and that help your community or the people you love, or the things you care about will in return help you boost your self-esteem and will change the way you look at yourself. If you invest your time in activities that help others, you will not only help yourself but you will participate in creating a better place for other individuals as well. For example if you invest in some activities which are charitable, for example organizing some event that will help raise money for the poor or for someone who is suffering from a disease, or you simply volunteer in your local soup kitchen and help homeless people you will benefit in so many ways.

First, you will get to enjoy the satisfaction, the fulfillment that comes from helping others. Second, you will actively participate in making this world a better place and helping your society to improve and become a better place. Third, you will change the way you look at yourself, you will no longer be a person who spends their free time lying around or being lazy, but you will see yourself as a person who is amazing and who does something and helps the society. Last, people will also notice your behavior and will start appreciating what you are doing.

Volunteering can also do wonders for your professional life, too. Donating your time can teach you a new skill, help add something special to your résumé, and allow you to meet new connections with similar interests as you.

If you are in your twenties or early thirties then you are in what many people call the "formative years" because this is the time of your life when you form habits that will carry out through the rest of your life. That is why it is crucial to focus on life skills that you need to master to live a better life. These skills can range from patience and dealing with rejection to living within your means and being an overall better individual. Also this is the perfect time when you can spear a few hours per week to do some activities that you enjoy. Once you get married and start focusing on creating a family, building a home, you will have less time to focus on these activities so this is the perfect time to follow your heart and do the things you like.

It does not matter how old you are, what gender you are and what you like, every single one of us should be able to spare some time and do activities that help us stay healthy. So many of us take health for granted`, and only when we get sick do we start to appreciate our health. Well, as the years pass by, we begin to lose our health and vitality so we should all start doing activities whose purpose is to help us stay healthy. Go for a run, or get a gym membership, join the club and try playing a sport you've love since childhood, or simply go for a walk. Even taking a course that explains to you how to live a healthy life or how to prepare healthy meals counts as an activity with purpose – it helps you become a better person.

Another activity that you can pursue that will help you grow and develop is an activity that is mentally stimulating you. One of the biggest mistakes that each one of us has made in some period of their life is forgetting to take care of their mental health. And our mental health is as important as our physical health if not even more important. These type of activities can easily become your favorite hobby because they will help you develop your creativity, stay sharp and at the same time they will relax you. So start doing some activities such as playing crossword games, or solving puzzles. They will help you reduce everyday stress and at the same time, they will keep you on your toes.

Some of the other activities that are meaningful and purposeful and will help you grow as a human beings are: reading, travelling, learning new things and saving for the future. With reading and learning new things you are broadening your horizon, you are improving your memory you are changing the way you think and you are growing mentally. Traveling on the other hand is a great thing you can do. Although traveling and saving cannot really be classified as activities, they sure are meaningful and purposeful and will do wonders for you. Travel is our way of experiencing the world. Traveling are small adventures, happy and fun trips that become memories and stories that are worth telling. It can make life richer with memories, richer with experience, richer with knowledge, richer with stories, and richer with friendships. Traveling can be good for both your soul and your heart. It will inspire you, leave you speechless and then turn you into a storyteller. Spare some money every month and once a year go somewhere where you have never been before. Let the world present itself to you. Open yourself to new experiences, to new people and new love. Once you experience the sweet taste of travel, you will never be the same. You will end up being addicted to it.

We also mentioned saving. Yes, it is not an activity but it sure is meaningful and purposeful. In life, everything changes in a blink of an eye, and you can never know what tomorrow will hold for you. So having some money aside can never hurt you.

The last meaningful activity we will mention is socializing. Every once in a while, do something social, something that is outside your comfort zone. If you are a bookworm, organize a trip with your friends or go camping. If you are shy, organize karaoke and surprise everyone. If you are adventurous, find another type of adventure – join a book club or a movie club. You will never know, maybe one of these activities will eventually grow to your heart and you will end up loving it. Join a dance class, go bowling, get a car club membership, join your local women's empowerment group and say goodbye to anxiety. Growing your circle of loved ones and spending time with them is not something you will regret, it is something that will help you feel better and will give your life more meaning.

Time to reflect

➢ What activities do you participate in during your spare time? How meaningful are they to you? What is their purpose?

➢ What activities would you like to try?

➢ Is there something stopping you from trying new activities? If yes, then how can you overcome those fears, obstacles?

Learning to grow and being ok with getting support and help

This chapter sums up everything we have talked about, and a little more. The purpose of this entire book is to teach you how to grow, how to stop being afraid of your true potential, how to start valuing yourself, to see your qualities, how to value them and start working on yourself. It is a guide on how to deal with everyday situations that bring you down and how to focus on the things that really matter in your life: valuing yourself, setting goals, working on them and participating in meaningful activities that help you grow.

Learning how to grow is not easy. It is a lifelong process. It is something that happens to you on a daily basis whether you are aware of that or not. If you don't believe me, stop for a second and think. Think about yourself five years ago. Can you say that you are exactly the same person as you were then? Can you say that absolutely nothing has changed in you? Of course not. You have changed physically, you have met some new people, and you have learned some new skills, you have also experienced something new and that's the beauty of life. That's amazing!!

Learning to grow means learning how to adjust in a society that is changing every second. It means learning how to deal with new situations, with new people. Learning to grow means accepting yourself for who you are and forgiving yourself. Forgiveness is crucial part of learning how to grow because it brings you inner peace and sets you free. By forgiving you aren't only helping the person whom you forgive but you're also helping yourself to close that chapter of your life and move on. On the other hand, by forgiving yourself, you're getting rid of the anger, of the fear, of the resentment in your heart and you are making space for love. You're growing into a stronger person who values itself. You're starting to love yourself and that is one of the hardest tasks each one of us has to learn how to do. You can't love others if you don't love yourself first. Also how can others love you if you don't love yourself? Growing means standing on the ground firmly, meeting with your past, analyzing your mistakes, looking in to the eyes of your fears of your demons and accepting that you have made mistakes. It means taking responsibility for your actions, and being big enough to apologize to others and to hold yourself accountable about the things you have done and the pain you have caused. There's no one who hasn't made a mistake. With taking responsibility for your actions, you're showing that you're a better person than you were before and you're opening the doors of your heart, you're opening the doors of forgiveness. Once you forgive yourself, you start to discover new things. You stop being afraid that you will make mistakes in front of others because you realize that you will eventually make them but it is ok because it is only human to make them. Growing also means understanding that every action has its own reaction. Growing also means understanding that not reacting is also an action by itself, and it is also a decision and as such, it has an impact on your life. Learning to grow means learning about yourself, knowing your strengths and weaknesses, working on them and creating yourself. Growing means accepting who you are, not being afraid of your uniqueness and becoming the person you desire to be. It means setting goals high and valuing yourself. It means reflecting regularly on who you are, listening to your own instincts for improvement. Growing up means knowing when to fight and when it is not worth it. It means knowing which fights you can win and which you should surrender. Growing up means accepting the fact that sometimes you will need help and support and it is ok to ask someone to give them to you.

We aren't born to live a lonely life. As human beings we all need support and help for the others to survive. Some people rely on religious beliefs to help overcome obstacles and others rely on the support and help from loved ones. When we were kids, we needed the help from our parents our grandparents to learn the basics of our life. Their help and support helped us to make the first steps to learn the first words. When we grew up and became teenagers, we needed the help of our friends to survive the changes that were happening to our body, and our mind. With their support and help we have gone through some nasty first break ups, we have learned tough life lessons that we should not trust everyone blindly. Later, with the love of our life, support of our friends and help of our family we have made the first steps into society. So why is it so difficult for some of us to understand that it is ok to ask for help? I don't mean that you should relay entirely on the support and help of other people to go through life, but rather that you should make a balance and know when to go alone and do things on your own and when to ask for help and support.

Probably the biggest problem that we face when we ask for support and help is vulnerability. We have this wrong idea in our heads that we should be able to do everything on our own and that admitting that we need someone's help may somehow make us look or be weak. That is not the case. Being able to ask for help and support when it is really needed is a sign of strength not weakness.

How can you ask for help and support without being afraid of being judged? Needing help with dealing with an issue is very common. Individuals sometime need assistance from an individual who has trained in the specialty area of counseling. Seeking professional help can allow you an outlet to express your feelings and help you get an understanding of how to deal with feelings.

Also, remember that just as you need other people's support and help, they also need yours so be generous with giving your support to others. Spare some of your time to help them and do not add attachments to it. Help because you want to help not because you expect something in return from them. Finally, be easy to support. This means when someone offers to help you, accept their help and let them help you in their way. A lot of times we don't know how to support one another so we do what we feel is right. Lastly you need to learn how to accept help – be open about their feedback and comments and take into consideration their opinions and advice.

Time to reflect

➤ Look at the past year or two. How much do you think you have grown?

➤ Be honest with yourself. Are you satisfied with your growth? What do you want to change in your character? What is stopping your growth?

➢ Do you find it difficult to ask for help and support? If yes, then what do you think, why you find it difficult to ask for help?

Conclusion

They key to living healthy life is being mentally strong enough to deal with everything that life throws at you. Moreover, being mentally healthy does not mean always being in a perfect condition and not letting anything touch you. That is simply not possible because we are all humans and as such we all go through life facing disappointments, loss and change. The only difference is that happy, mentally strong people know hot to bounce back from the punches that life throws at them. They know how to stay strong, deal with stress, value themselves and deal with traumas from their past.

Mentally strong people know their true potential, they do not lie to themselves, and they know precisely who they are, what their strength and weaknesses are, and how important it is to not forget about yourself. These people possess the knowledge and tools required for coping with difficult situations. They know how to go in a fight with life and get out of it as winners with a smile on their face. They know that life is simply a mixture of bad and good moments and what really matters is staying truthful to yourself, remaining focused, calm, flexible and productive. They know that whatever life throws at them, they will be able to deal with it because they believe in themselves. They know who they are and what they want. They aren't afraid to go after the things their heart desires and at the same time, they aren't ashamed to ask for support and help from other people.

Mentally strong people believe in themselves and they know that every problem has a solution and that sooner or later that solution will present itself. Mentally strong people are the people we all should strive to be. Not forgetting about yourself and what you have the potential to be and accomplish is key!

Made in the USA
Middletown, DE
15 April 2017